On the Wide Roads of Mumbai

One Orphan's Journey from a Christian Orphanage to the Streets of Mumbai and Back

by Alex Sam
with Sarah Bass

Copyright @2015 by Alex Sam

All rights reserved. No part of this book may be reproduced in any form by any electronic or mechanical means including information storage or retrieval systems – for example, electronic, photocopy, recording – without the prior written permission of the author. The only exception is brief quotations in printed reviews.

Acknowledgments

I want to acknowledge the incredible role several persons have played in my life to make this book possible.

First and foremost, I acknowledge the Lord Jesus Christ, He has changed my life and still He is on work, may He receive all glory and honor.

Second, I want to acknowledge persons who have greatly influenced my life through their love and care, Dr. M. A. Thomas & Mrs. Ammini Thomas, Dr. Sam George & Elizabeth Sam, Dr. Samuel A. Thomas & Shelley Thomas, Mr. P. V. Thomas & Family, Mr. Bhagirath & Family, Mr. V.S.Thomas & Family, Mr. John (Babuji) & family, Bro. Trevor D. Linares & Family, Bro. Mathews Vattiprolu & Family and many more (I might have to write another book for same)!

Third, I would like to thank Sarah Bass, the actual author of the book, who took her valuable time to pen my life in the form of book; I have been praying for these from many years, finally she helped me to make this dream happen.

Last but not the least; I would like to thank my lovely wife Sunita (Janu). She chooses to marry me in spite all weakness in me, she has been used far more than she will ever know to make me more social, effective leader and humble. Janu, thanks for your continuous encouragement, prayers, rebuke and word of confirmation.

Endorsements

"The Wide Roads of Mumbai is a moving biography, made all the more piercing by its spare, clear-eyed language. But this book is also theology -- not offering words that explain obscure passages, but rather vibrant windows that help us see what over-familiar biblical truths actually look like experienced amidst ache and hope, celebration and sorrow."
--Jedd Medefind, President, Christian Alliance for Orphans and author of Becoming Home

" Pastor Alex has hosted two of our Health Teams International mission trips to India over the last 10 years. In that capacity we have found him to be a wonderful man of God with the utmost in integrity, ingenuity and resourcefulness. His ministry is having a significant lasting impact on the lives of those he leads and cares for. I am proud to call Alex my friend."

-Dr. Tom J. Harle
President Health Teams International (Canada)

"In June 2012 our family visited mr Alex Sam in his home town to meet him and to get to know the ministry. Since then we've followed up the work that goes on in Pakur, India, and we've been in regular contact with him.

Based on our experiences we've seen that mr Alex Sam is truly devoted to his work for the benefit of the children. It's very clear that he wants to help orphans and this is his driving motive for all he does.

An important matter that I greatly respect is that mr Alex Sam wants to educate the orphans and also his workers. I agree with him that education is one of the main keys to better life for each person and also benefits the community by preparing knowledgeable people to take responsibility and leadership.

For a westerner India alone is an overwhelming experience. Taking care of orphans there has many challenges starting with every-day-issues to administration and economy. Despite of the challenges we met happy children who were together like a family. I respect the strength of mr Alex Sam navigating through problems without burdening the children.

The ministry has never been receiving regular financial support and it's a miracle that it's been running and growing for years. Mr Alex Sam's goal is to make the functions more self supporting which is a great goal. Together with regular and budgeted financial support the work has a huge potential!"

-Jesaja Arola, Pilot

"First I like to open this testimony on behalf of Everette Mission by saying to God be he glory Great things He hath done!

I have been privileged to be part Of Alex and Sunita"s lives for over a decade now. Both of them and their family as well as there work with children have found a special place in my heart.

I praise Jesus for the opportunity to be part of the great things they are doing in Pakur! As they started their ministry with humble beginnings, it has grown over the past several years to a God-sized ministry. They are a blessing to so many in their area. My family and I have been able to spend time with them on various occasions and view their work first hand.

I can honestly say that the children's home as well as the schools they run are awesome. The Lord has surely used Alex and Sunita to be a bless the people of Jharkhand with great education, great safe-havens, and above the Truth of Gods love!

We have been able to share our love and gifts to the kids on different occasions and each time I received more of a blessing than I have given to them, or at least I leave with that impression each time. We always enjoy the chance to be part of their lives! Their work is well noticed by the people of their city and not only there but state-wide and nationally. I am thankful for the burden that Jesus has given to Alex and Sunita to run the ministry right! So many in the country run unregistered homes, I am thankful they are doing things right! They are certain a worthy cause to invest in, that is if you'd like to invest in the life to come.

May they continue to grow and may God expand their ministry to an uncountable accomplishment. He is using them to bring awareness to people not only in India but in several other countries as well! Please remember their work and if the Lord in heaven leads you, please

give. They have reached a great need to build and expand their work. May you and I continue to be part in this Jabez type ministry!
Alex and Sunita and all the kids of pakur, we love you all and pray we may meet again before we reach our eternal home!
Headed to heaven!"

-Dr. Todd Payne
Pastor, Speaker, Missionary

Dedication

This book is dedicated to Dr. M. A. Thomas, well known as PAPA (Father), man with vision to raise, equip one million children, he was father for thousands of orphan kids including me, and apart from him I would like to dedicate this book to all who are involved in orphan care, foster care movement throughout the globe.

I admire your love, faith and your courage to raise orphan, abandoned and vulnerable children like me,
my prayer is that God will use you to raise up a new generation of leaders, preachers, teachers and
more from these kids.

Table of Contents

Acknowledgements

Endorsements

Dedication

Chapter 1: Orphaned

Chapter 2: Emmanuel Orphanage

Chapter 3: Fleeing

Chapter 4: Mumbai

Chapter 5: Criminal

Chapter 6: Prodigal Son

Chapter 7: Bible College

Chapter 8: Sunita

Chapter 9: Bilara

Chapter 10: Kota

Chapter 11: Abraham

Chapter 12: Varanasi

Chapter 13: Call Center Then Called Back

Chapter 14: Pakur

Chapter 15: Orphans

Chapter 16: The Body of Christ

Chapter 17: Everett Mission

Chapter 18: Down the Road

Chapter 19: Thy Kingdom Come

Chapter 20: Final Words

Chapter 1: Orphaned

There are two accounts of how I came to be an orphan. One says that I was an infant; the other says I was a small child. The truth is, I don't know which one is true because there is no record. Not of me, my mother, or my father. Either way, I must have been small.

The story I've come to accept is that I was born on March 20, 1981. When I was six months old, my mother died of tuberculosis. When I was nine months old, God caused me to be brought to the Emmanuel Orphanage in Kota, Rajasthan, where I was handed over to the Orphanage's care. A few weeks after I was brought to Emmanuel, it became known that my father had died. They say that it was my father who brought me to the orphanage, but no one is really certain.

"I will not leave you as orphans; I will come to you." - John 14:18 (ESV)

Chapter 2: Emmanuel Orphanage

I don't remember much of my life in the orphanage as a small child, but that is where I grew up. For a while, I was very good in Sunday school, paying attention to the teachings, singing with all my heart and meeting all of the spiritual expectations. I was very good. But, despite all of this, there was a feeling deep down inside of me that began to fill me slowly, slowly, slowly...

It was the feeling of being unloved.

In India, there are two types of orphans. First, there are orphans like me who have no parents and no family. There is another type of orphan, however, who does have family members: a mother and no father, a father and no mother, or he or she has both, but are living in a situation so poor, their parents can't support the child. Sometimes the parents are lepers. These parents still want their children to be educated, however, so they are brought to an orphanage. Yet, they still have interaction with their kids - sometimes once a year, sometimes once every two years, and if they live close, sometimes every six months. It depends on the ability of the parents to travel.

I had friends at Emmanuel, but most of them were not real orphans. And even though they were not living with their parents, they still have the privilege of getting new clothes now and then, receiving sweets and chocolates and other edible things, and occasionally going on vacation. As a ten-year-old boy, when I saw the things the other children received, I was envious. I would approach them and say, "If you share your things with me, you are a good person."

If they didn't share their things with me, I would tell them, "One of these nights, your suitcase may have a break-in."

I didn't understand it. Why didn't I have such privileges? Where were my new clothes and sweets? I didn't have any, because my parents were dead. That was one of the reasons why I ended up rebelling.

In Emmanuel's effort to discipline us, we would often receive heavy punishment. Even today, I feel that, despite my behavior (which did warrant discipline), many times it was excessive. People say that such heavy discipline changes your life, but really, only Jesus can bring about true and lasting change.

I was often disciplined for losing my books in school, or not showing up for morning prayers, or skipping class to go to a movie. For this I would be harshly disciplined. As a result, I began running away. I didn't just run away once; I ran away from the orphanage many times. Whenever they found me and brought me back, I felt more and more like I was in a prison I couldn't leave.

> "Where shall I go from your Spirit? Or where shall I flee from your presence? If I ascend to heaven, you are there! If I make my bed in Sheol, you are there! If I take the wings of the morning and dwell in the uttermost parts of the sea, even there your hand shall lead me, and your right hand shall hold me. If I say, 'Surely the darkness shall cover me, and the light about me be night,' even the darkness is not dark to you; the night is

bright as the day, for darkness is as light with you… For you formed my inward parts; you knitted me together in my mother's womb. I praise you, for I am fearfully and wonderfully made. Wonderful are your works; my soul knows it very well. My frame was not hidden from you, when I was being made in secret, intricately woven in the depths of the earth. Your eyes saw my unformed substance; in your book were written, every one of them, the days that were formed for me, when as yet there was none of them." -Psalm 139: 7-16

Chapter 3: Fleeing

There was a boy in the orphanage by the name or Suresh Sawant. One vacation, Suresh went to visit his relatives' home, and when he came back he had a suitcase full of new clothes.

One day, I went to Suresh and asked him if I could wear one of his outfits on Sunday for the day, so I could go to church in them.

"No," he said to me.

He wasn't planning on wearing them either, because they were new things. He just kept them folded in his suitcase, which he kept carefully tucked away.

Finally, by the time I was eleven-years-old, I was fed up. I had had enough of life at the orphanage. I made up my mind to run away for good, and to go where I couldn't be found. So, the day I decided to make my escape, I went into Suresh's room, took his suitcase (with his four sets of brand new clothes in it) and left Emmanuel.

As usual, when it was discovered that I had run away again, the Emmanuel Bible students came behind me looking for me, so I ran to the train station. While in the station, I caught sight of some of the Bible students there, so I quickly boarded a train and locked myself in the bathroom stall on one of the railway cars. People came and knocked on the door, and I thought they were the Bible students, so I didn't open it.

I spent fourteen hours locked in that railway bathroom. It was nasty, but after the first two hours, I got used to the smell. I was more afraid of how I'd be disciplined if the Bible students got hold of me.

Fourteen hours later, when I finally built up the courage to unlock the bathroom stall and open the door, I nearly fell over in shock. I was in Mumbai.

"O Lord, you have searched me and known me! You know when I sit down and when I rise up; you discern my thoughts from afar. You search out my path and my lying down
and are acquainted with all my ways. Even before a word is on my tongue, behold, O Lord, you know it

altogether. You hem me in, behind and before, and lay your hand upon me. Such knowledge is too wonderful for me; it is high; I cannot attain it."

-Psalm 139:1-6

Chapter 4: Mumbai

I had never seen such big buildings before. I had never been out of my orphanage. When I had run away in times past, it had always been to the small surrounding village towns. But here, in Mumbai, I had never seen such buildings and such crowds. In the train station, people were walking shoulder to shoulder, coming and going, to and fro from work and this place and that place. Being such a small boy, I was afraid to walk between all those people, because I thought I would surely be trampled. So, I sat in the train station for two days, eating nothing.

Then one day, a man came up to me. He had a briefcase in his hand. "Would you like to carry this for me?" he asked.

I looked at the suitcase. "No," I replied.

"I will give you money," he said.

I didn't know at the time that that was one of the ways I could make money in the railway station. Plus, I was hungry and in need of food. "Yes," I said, changing my mind.

The man's briefcase was medium size, but it was heavy – too heavy, in fact, for me to lift, because I was weak from not having eaten in days.

The man, watching me struggle, had pity on me. He took the briefcase back and gave me ten rupees.

"Go and buy yourself something to eat," he said. So I took the money and went to the railway canteen and bought myself a meal. To this day, I consider that man a noble man because of the compassion he had on me.

Soon after that, I met some other boys similar to me in age and situation, and we got together and started begging in the train station for a living. Sometimes we would do odd-and-end jobs like mop the trains and sweep the cars, and people would give us some food or money. Every train has a coach called a pantry car, and we would go to it, help the attendant with something, and receive food in return. Sometimes, we would outright break into the food car and take all of the eatable stuffs!

Food wasn't a problem for us children. It was money we found ourselves most in need of. Whatever money we managed to get from begging would be stolen from us by a gang of older boys who would beat us up as the end of a day and steal it.

At that time, I was only eleven. After begging for six or seven months, I was caught by the police and thrown into beggars' prison. Police do this in an attempt to reduce the amount of begging on the streets and in the train stations of Mumbai. Even though those in beggars' prison aren't technically criminals, and the jailers still feed you, it isn't good food and there are no baths. The conditions are nasty. Jail life is no life.

I was in beggars' prison for nearly three months. When I was finally let out, I went to a branch of Emmanuel Orphanage in Tenkasi. I stayed in that orphanage for a few months, but the same thing happened. I received very heavy discipline. One night, the headmistress there, whom I'd become accustomed to calling "Ma," woke me up in the middle of sleep and confronted me for taking something from another believer's home.

But it wasn't true. Had I ever done such things? Yes, I had. But I didn't steal from the person she said I had stolen from.

Nevertheless, there in the middle of the night she disciplined me severely. Perhaps she thought it was for my own good, but I couldn't take it anymore. I ran away that very night.

I knew of only one other place to go: an institute in south India by the name of Bible Bhavan. I knew a couple of good people, Mr. and Mrs. Chrian, who owned a printing press, so I went there to live and work with them. I learned more of the Bible there, and I had a home with them where I was loved. But, by then, running had become a habit for me, and I missed living a free life on the streets. So, even though I could have stayed with that couple, after three months I hopped on another train, grabbed a broom, and that was my fare from south to west India. I went back to Mumbai.

When I returned to Mumbai, I was a little older than when I first went - now thirteen going on fourteen. I reunited with old friends, and we went back to our old ways, cleaning and collecting money. We walked in traffic, polishing people's car mirrors and things, then asking for money, and they would give it to us. But, yet again, the older boys on the street posed a problem for us, as they continued to beat us and steal our money.

One night, after such a robbery, I sat in the train station and cried. It was then that I remembered someone telling me, "If you are to live, you must know how to hit, and hit hard."

Upon remembering that, I saw an iron rod near where I was sitting on the track. So I went, picked up the rod, and ran after the boy who'd robbed me. I beat him with all my might and took back my money – all the money he had in his pocket, in fact.

The next day, I was caught by the police and put into criminal jail. That is where my life changed. I became confident, for the first time, that I could do things by myself. I could take care of myself. Nobody could come and snatch my money anymore. While in jail, I learned many things; that there are people who will employ you to beat up others and then pay you for it. I learned that you can snatch things in the dark if you have the confidence. In jail, I became a criminal.

"All we like sheep have gone astray; we have turned – every one – to his own way; and the LORD has laid on him the iniquity of us all.
He was oppressed, and he was afflicted, yet he opened not his mouth; like a lamb that is led to the slaughter, and like a sheep that before its shearers is silent, so he

opened not his mouth. By oppression and judgment he was taken away; and as for his generation, who considered that he was cut off out of the land of the living, stricken for the transgressions of my people? And they made his grave with the wicked and with a rich man in his death, although he had done no violence, and there was no deceit in his mouth..." -Isaiah 53:6-9

Chapter 5: Criminal

I was in jail for five or six days. When I was released, I began my criminal life, and ended up, at the age of fourteen, in a child gang.

It is amazing how, when you are a beggar, nobody is with you. Nobody sees you. But as soon as people see that they can make use of you, they will bring you out of the shadows.

People used us to handle drugs for them. I used to take things from one place to another. I never knew who I worked for, or where those who had me transport it were. It was the sort of thing to where I would get a package from one place and then would be told where to take it.

In addition to selling drugs, three or four other friends and I began selling pornography at the railway station. We would first get them from shops. People selling the books would come to us and we would take orders, supply, and get the start-up money from them. From there, we would go and sell the books. We made a lot of money doing it. That's how we survived. When I think about it now, it's sobering, but then, while I was doing it, I enjoyed it.

When I became a street vendor, selling things on trains (we only sold porn sometimes), we would sell anything we could find to sell: books, calculators, key chains, radios, suitcases, pens. Anything we could find cheaply, we would buy and then turn around and sell. We sold on local trains, railway bridges, at traffic signals and on railway platforms. Many times, on the train platforms, there was such a rush of people getting on and off, you could take money from somebody's pocket and they would never know it. So we did that also.

I loved the freedom to do whatever I wanted with nobody there to stop me. No one to tell me what I can do and what I'm not allowed to do. I really enjoyed those days.

In fights, I always won. Many times, when you see a person alone, a child by himself cannot go and fight with him. But when there are ten or twelve of you with arms - sticks, swords and knives - you can rob a single person very easily. That's what my gang did.

While living on the streets of Mumbai, I had many "houses." All the railways stations were my home. Street lights and traffic signals as well. Those of us in the gang would sleep on the ground, wherever we could find a space. When it rained, it was more difficult, but we found places under the railway bridges. In some stations, there are dry water tanks, so we would sleep there. But when the police found us, they would beat us for trespassing, and also because they suspected that we were doing things that we weren't supposed to do.

At this point in my life, I wouldn't call myself a non-believer; I believed in the Lord because I accepted Jesus as my Savior while at the orphanage in Tenkasi. I took baptism, and tried to live a good life. But, we are human, and make errors. The punishments I would receive for those errors, however, did not seem fair and fitting to me, and as a result, I backslid.

I was not interested in talking about God at that time anyway. I didn't understand why - why is it that, even though I accepted Jesus as my personal Savior, I was going through so much hardship and difficulty?

There was a point in my life when I figured all religions were the same; people just made a business out of it. Nevertheless, while living in Mumbai, I would frequent the churches and temples and mosques, because there they would give out free food. I wouldn't stay for the worship; I just went to eat. As worshippers would leave their shoes outside the temples and mosques when they went inside to pray, I would also steal a pair of shoes, leaving the person to walk home barefoot.

There was a slum church in Mumbai that I would attend occasionally, not because I was a "Christian," but because I wanted to leave an impression. I would show up just to let the people in the church know that I was a big shot in the city, a successful street boy and one of the rulers of Mumbai.

Even so, the pastor there, Pastor Shekhar, would always take time to sit with me and give me counsel about the life I was living. During those conversations I would think to myself, "Okay, here is this man beginning his lecture to me." I would sit there and listen so as not to disrespect him, because the truth is, I did respect him. I just never did anything he advised me to do. Rather, I respected him because he was a good man, and even though he knew the kind of life I was living, he allowed me to stay in his home sometimes and his wife would cook nice food for me. While on the streets, I knew that there were one or two places I could call home, and one or two people I could call "Uncle" and "Auntie," and their home was one. The Shekhars were good people.

Street boys in Mumbai have particular areas to manage and particular jobs to do in the city. Mumbai is so big, we would have our own section that belonged to us. Among the things we would do was something called "fielding," which is how we went about beating up a single person. The person would be walking on the street, and unbeknownst to him, he would be surrounded on all corners by our gang, so that he wouldn't have the chance to run when we jumped him. We would do this often on the wide roads of Mumbai. There are times we hurt people seriously, doing who knows what kind of damage, and then we would run, because there were so many places in the city, nobody would be able to find us.

There was a brief period during my criminal life in Mumbai when I went back to Kota. I was about fifteen years old. I didn't go to Emmanuel Orphanage, though; I just stayed in the city. But even then, something happened and I ended up in jail for three months for beating someone up. As soon as those three months were over, instead of going back to the orphanage, I ran back to Mumbai. My heart had become so stubborn. Everyone has a day though, and my day was coming.

Yet it was the will of the LORD to crush him; he has put him to grief; when his soul makes an offering for guilt, he shall see his offspring; he shall prolong his days; the will of the LORD shall prosper in his hand. Our of the anguish of his soul he shall see and be satisfied; by his knowledge shall the righteous one, my servant, make many to be accounted righteous, and he shall bear their iniquities. Therefore I will divide him a portion with the many, and he shall divide the spoil with the strong, because he poured out his soul to death and was numbered with the transgressors; yet he bore the sins of many, and makes intercession for the transgressors."

-Isaiah 53:10-12

Chapter 6: Prodigal Son

Being in a child gang, we made so much money that after buying food and clothing, we had enough to go and sleep with women. There are many places in Mumbai that are known for prostitution; even on the open streets, there are many willing girls. So when we saw a girl we wanted, we would take her and go in the train or somewhere like that. Having so much money, we had everything, and that included the girls. It became a daily routine for me.

And then, two of my friends died from AIDS. They were strong, healthy boys, but it was all of the prostitution that killed them. When I heard that, I was so afraid. I went and took an AIDS test, and thank God I didn't have AIDS; even during that time, God was looking out for me, and I had sense enough to take more precautions than the others. Nevertheless, it scared me. I was terrified for my life, and finally realized that I was not on the right path. The two of my friends who had died had ended horribly. They were not believers, and living on the street, they didn't have any family. So, when they died, people took their bodies to machines and burned them.

Growing up in a Christian environment, the idea of being burned was not an agreeable one to me. I thought to myself, "If I die, will there be someone to bury me? To care for me and make the necessary arrangements? What will be my future?"

At the age of sixteen, I started thinking hard about all these things, even while still roaming the streets. I hadn't yet given up that life, but the seed was in my mind, and it stayed there. I began to think that perhaps there was a better life I could be living than the one I knew now. Maybe there was a different road; a better road.

Around this time, I went to Bharuch in Gujarat, where one of the senior orphan boys with whom I had grown up, T.M. Onkar, had started a mission with his wife (an American lady), Rebecca. When I went to visit his home, I thought to myself, "This boy grew up in the same orphan home that I did. Now, he is married, and has a school, and is living such a good life. How good that would be."

In talking with him, he said, "Alex, why don't you go back to Emmanuel Orphanage and study there? They will keep you."

I told him yes, I would, but upon leaving him I returned to Mumbai, because in truth, my mind was getting there but I still wasn't convinced. I was struggling internally about whether to go back, because in Mumbai I was doing well money wise, I was doing well power-wise, and I was enjoying the freedom I was living. Even when I would bring up the idea of possibly going back to the orphanage to some of my street friends, they would ask me why, when I was living such a good, enviable life?

"People are afraid of you," they said. "If you walk up to any group of boys, they will run away from you."

Hearing this always boosted my confidence, and made me think that yes, I wanted to keep my life on the street.

But finally, one day, I decided. I went to the slum church and found out that there was to be a church inauguration conducted by Pastor A.M. Mathew, and none other than Dr. M.A. Thomas, the president of Emmanuel Orphanage, and his son, Dr. Samuel Thomas, were coming to the church for the ceremony.

"Well then," I thought to myself. "Let me go and meet them and see what happens."

So, on the inauguration day, I went. There I was, a thin boy with long hair and a thick belt with a motorcycle chain through it, knives and cigarette packets stuffed in my pockets, standing in the back of the church while Dr. M.A. Thomas was preaching.

Right there, in the middle of Dr. Thomas's message, he paused and said, "Everyone, I am so happy to see one of my sons here!"

With that, he brought me to the front of the church; me - dirty, nasty, and probably smelling - and he put his arm around me and said with a smile in front of everyone, "This boy is one of my sons, who grew up in the orphanage, and is now living in Mumbai. I am so happy he came to see me."

That broke my heart. Here I was, living a nasty life, a life not worth anything, and yet here it was, this big, important man, this big shot, calling me his son in front of all those people...

When the meeting was over, I didn't go close to Dr. M.A. Thomas, because I didn't want him to touch me and feel the cigarettes and knives in my pockets. I ran out of the church, and there I saw Dr. Samuel Thomas. I went up to him.

"Could I come back?" I asked him, regarding returning to the orphanage. It was all talk at the time, but I still asked.

"Yes, you can come back," he said.

But I didn't go back. I stayed in Mumbai. It wasn't until months later, when I was selling things on a train one day, that I happened to see Dr. Samuel Thomas again.

"Do you know me?" I asked him.

"Alex!" he said.

I then asked him the same question. "Could I come back?"

"Yes, anytime," he replied.

This time, I decided I would go. It took two or three months to finally make up my mind, because I was already nearly eighteen years old. But I went anyway, to see what would happen and what the response would be. I thought to myself that if it didn't happen the way I hoped, I could always leave and return to Mumbai.

The day I left, I didn't tell any of the street boys or my people in Mumbai. I just left. When I reached Emmanuel Orphanage, I went to the office. I wanted to go inside, but I couldn't bring myself to do it. I just stood there.

One of the big brothers in the orphanage, Trevor De Linares, was working on staff that day, saw me and brought me inside. Trevor was a good man, and always one to help me.

We went in to Dr. Samuel Thomas's office. When Dr. Thomas saw me, he looked at Trevor and said, "What do you think? Should we keep him?" I think he was having a little fun. I stood there nervously awaiting his answer.

Bhaiya Trevor said, "Yes. We should keep him. I will take responsibility for him."

And that is how I came back. I repented, and re-surrendered my life to Jesus.

"There was a man who had two sons. And the younger of them said to his father, 'Father, give me the share of property that is coming to me.' And he divided his property between them. Not many days later, the younger son gathered all he had and took a journey into a far country, and there he squandered his property in reckless living. And when he had spent everything, a severe famine arose in that country, and he began to be in need. So he went and hired himself out to one of the citizens of that country, who sent him into his fields to feed the pigs. And he was longing to be fed with the pods that the pigs ate, and no one gave him anything. "But when he came to himself, he said, 'How many of my father's hired servants have more than enough bread, but I perish here with hunger! I will arise and go to my father, and I will say to him, 'Father, I have sinned against heaven and before you. I am no longer worthy to be called your son. Treat me as one of your hired servants.' And he arose and came to his father. But while he was still a long way off, his father saw him and felt compassion, and ran and embraced him and kissed him. And the son said to him, 'Father, I have sinned against heaven and before you. I am no longer worthy to be called your son.' But the father said to his servants, 'Bring the best robe, and put it on him, and put a ring on his hand, and shoes on his feet. And bring the fatted calf and kill it, and let us eat and celebrate. For this my son was dead and is alive again; he was lost, and is found.' -Luke 15:11-24

Chapter 7: Bible College

Being almost 18 upon my return, I couldn't go back to study in school. The question was, what was I going to do?

Initially I thought I would end up working in the printing press, or doing office work, but when they asked me what I wanted to do, I told them that I wanted to study. I think even those at Emmanuel wanted to see what my potential was.

I was therefore sent to a ten-week Bible course at Emmanuel Bible College in Delhi. When I arrived at the Bible College, there were many degree-holders and people with high school certificates studying there, and here I was, a young man with no formal education, only just knowing how to read and write. Nevertheless, I had a good understanding of God's Word, and as a result I did well in that short-term class.

After I completed the course, I returned to the Emmanuel Institute and went to see Trevor again (the same Trevor De Linares with whom I'd grown up in the orphanage).

"Bhaiya," I said. "Can I study more at length in the Bible College?"

Understanding my situation, he told me that yes, I could continue my studies. So I had a discussion with the chairman, and the College allowed me to begin my studies in the 2nd rather than the 1st year, and gave me the support I needed to stay there.

That was tremendous for me. I finished well and graduated. But, even then, I still wondered what it was that I was going to do with my life. I thought perhaps I would be considered for clerical work at the orphanage. The chairman of the College, however had other ideas. He told me that I was to teach at the College. In addition to that, he put me in charge of the Book Room, where we sell books and Bibles to students, and I was placed as the warden of the boys' hostel in the College living quarters.

That is how I started in the Lord's ministry. Many other students and I would go on gospel tours on weekends, traveling around and sharing the Gospel with local people. That was one of the events I enjoyed most, for I had the chance to organize young male and female students, bring them together, get on a bus and ride around distributing tracts. I loved it. Little did I know that the best was yet to come, because it was there, while working at the Bible College, that I met Sunita.

"I appeal to you therefore, brothers, by the mercies of God, to present your bodies as a living sacrifice, holy and acceptable to God, which is your spiritual worship. Do not be conformed to this world, but be transformed by the renewal of your mind, that by testing you may discern what is the will of God, what is good and acceptable and perfect."

-Romans 12:1-2

Chapter 8: Sunita

Sunita grew up in Emmanuel Orphanage - the same orphanage I did. I had known about her; I knew her name and that she was from Bihar, but I didn't know that she had parents until later.

Sunita is a wonderful singer. She was also the best girl in the orphanage. Children and workers and leaders alike loved her. She has such a beautiful spirit, and was always smiling. Her smile is one of the things she is best known for. So when I saw her, I thought to myself, "I think God wants her to be my wife."

In India, dating is not part of our culture, so there was no courtship between Sunita and me. When I noticed that she was all grown up and realized my interest in her, I made up my mind to talk to her.

So, one day, on a day the church members and staff went for a picnic in Chambal Garden, I made up my mind to take her aside and talk to her. Growing up as a street boy, I decided to give it to her straight.

"Sunita," I said, "I like you. Will you marry me?" There wasn't any "I love you" or anything at that time. I thought that I could only get one of two possible answers from her. Either she would say "no," or she would say "yes." In fact, however, I got neither.

What she said to me was equally straightforward. "You will have to talk to my parents."

"You have parents?" I asked, surprised.

"Yes," she answered. "They are in Bihar."

"Okay," I said. "We will talk."

Sunita happened to have an uncle by the name of Emmanuel Marandi working nearby, so I took Sunita to have our picture taken, gave it to him, paid for his train fare, and asked him to take the picture to Bihar to Sunita's parents, to show them that I was serious.

"Tell them that boy wants to marry girl, but girl wants your permission," I said. I respected Sunita for that, and don't regret it, because it showed me that she honored her parents in making decisions. I was very happy when Sunita's parents gave their consent.

Sunita and I still faced challenges, however, before we got married. Because Sunita worked at the time in the College President's kitchen, I went to him, told him that I loved Sunita and explained my intentions. He told me that all would be well, and not to worry, for he would help me in the arrangement of the necessary things.

Yet somewhere, something happened, and a great misunderstanding ensued, because soon after that, he came back to me and informed me that the College would not conduct our marriage. Furthermore, he dismissed Sunita from the Bible College, and sent for her uncle to escort her back to her family home in Bihar.

To this day, I don't know what happened. Some say that he said that Sunita broke the rules by consenting to have a photo taken with me. This doesn't make much sense, though, because I told him openly of my intentions, and he had agreed as a parent. I knew, however, that I had to marry Sunita soon, before she was sent back to her village, because once she was there, it would be difficult to marry her. For, in her tribe and culture, it is not within the tradition to marry an outsider. Those who do are labeled.

It had always been a dream of mine to marry during one of the conferences held at the Bible College. We held two every year. These conference times were special because pastors from all over India were in attendance, and as many of them knew me, they would be able to attend the wedding. Additionally, many pastors from other countries, including America, would come, and as I speak English, I would translate for them. During these times, it was common for love offerings to be given, and I knew that in order to start life with my wife, I needed money. I didn't have cooking vessels, or bed sheets, or pillows. I didn't have anything. I didn't even have a home. Therefore, I thought, yes, with my involvement and contribution, the Bible College would provide me with a family room as soon as I marry.

When I went to Dr. M.A. Thomas and asked him to conduct my marriage by his own hand, he said, "I want to, Alex. But I can't." He told me that his son didn't want it because, again, of some misunderstanding. Dr. Samuel Thomas had heard somewhere that I had said something against his family, which wasn't true, however he refused to consent. I still remember taking my mother-in-law, my wife's auntie and uncle to Dr. M.A. Thomas's chamber to ask. As much as he said he wanted to, however, he said he couldn't go against his son. I didn't know what to do or what to say about that.

Dr. M.A. Thomas was very gracious to me, though, because he called another senior pastor and requested that he conduct the ceremony, which he did. So, even though I felt as though there were blessings I missed because of that, I was grateful, and said, okay, well perhaps this is God's will. Because God always has His own way. He brought many good people into my life - senior pastors and all - and the pastor who officiated my wedding ceremony (his name was also Alex Sam, and he was from Bundi. Also present was Pastor Thomas Sam from Jhalawar), did a wonderful job. All of the details came together in the end, and it was good. So, on October 20th, 2002, Sunita and I were married; I was twenty and she was almost twenty-one.

"An excellent wife who can find?

She is far more precious than jewels.

The heart of her husband trusts in her,

And he will have no lack of gain.

-Proverbs 31:10-11

Chapter 9: Bilara

After Sunita and I were married, we were sent by the Emmanuel Institute to Bilara, in Jhodpur, for ministry. When Sunita and I got there, it was at the time of Diwali: the Hindu Holy Day. Upon our arrival, even though it is customary for a married couple to be given family quarters for residence, there were no rooms for us. We ended up being housed in some of the school rooms.

The school buildings where we worked were open buildings, so oftentimes the rooms Sunita and I were living in were also used half of the time for teachers' sitting rooms. During these times, our bedroom was separated from these public spaces by a single piece of plywood.

The space was very small. At night, when school was over, we were able to open up the whole space in the room, but during the day, we had to remain in the divided portion. We hardly had any privacy.

It was challenging for Sunita and me, because we were newly married, and upon arrival in Bilara, I only had 150 rupees in my hand (the equivalent of $3 in the United States). All of the money gifts I had received on our wedding day I had to allocate to pay for food, tents, and everything else needed for the ceremony. On top of that, we didn't know anyone, except one young boy: Bhaiju.

As we didn't have any bed sheets, Bhaiju gave us his so that we could sleep. Still, we didn't have pots or pans or any other cooking vessels for food.

I didn't know what to do, because I didn't have enough money to return to Kota. So, using the 150 rupees, we bought one meal a day to share. 150 rupees is nothing, though, so the money wouldn't even last four days. God works miracles though when we trust him all the way down to the end.

There was an American lady named Barbara who knew Sunita and me from Emmanuel. She passed by the orphanage for a visit, and upon speaking to Dr. M.A. Thomas, said, "I heard Sunita and Alex are married. Where are they?"

Dr. M.A. Thomas told her that we were in Bilara, and even though she was traveling to Pali, she decided to change her plans and come see Sunita and me.

She ended up visiting with us for two hours, during which time we had a meeting, fellowshipped and then prayed. After she left, Sunita came to me.

"Look at what Auntie left for us," she said. It was 1,000 rupees.

"Praise God!" I said.

With that money, we were able to purchase two pots, two plates, two cups, two spoons, and a kerosene stove. We were also able to go to a bed maker and pay down on a bed, because until then we had only been sleeping on a mattress. I explained that I would be able to pay off the bed in ten installments.

Fortunately, the bed makers had children studying in our school, so they were more than willing to help us. And that is how Sunita and I began. For six months, we stayed in that small school room, but it was tremendous, because God blessed us. I received a salary for working there in the ministry, running a small church in addition to the school. But, after a while, due to water issues in the area, I fell ill, and began to have problems with my legs. I eventually recovered, but nonetheless Dr. Thomas called us back to the headquarters in Kota.

"Therefore I tell you, do not be anxious about your life, what you will eat or what you will drink, nor about your body, what you will put on. Is not life more than food, and the body more than clothing? Look at the birds of the air: they neither sow nor reap nor gather into barns, and yet your heavenly Father feeds them. Are you not of more value than they? And which of you being anxious can add a single hour to his life? And why are you anxious about clothing? Consider the lilies of the field, how they grow: they neither toil nor spin, yet I tell you, even Solomon in all his glory was not arrayed like one of these. But if God so clothes the grass of the field, which today is alive and tomorrow is thrown into the oven, will he not much more clothe you, O you of little faith? Therefore do not be anxious, saying, 'What shall we eat?' or 'What shall we drink?' or 'What shall we wear?' For the Gentiles seek after all these things and your heavenly Father knows that you need them all. But seek first the kingdom of God and his righteousness, and all these things will be added to you." –Matthew 6:25-33

Chapter 10: Kota

When Sunita and I were called back to Kota, I was faced with a new set of challenges. Because I spent a good portion of my life on the roads of Mumbai, and Mumbai is known to have embraced much of western culture, I naturally embraced some of the cultural influences of the city. I enjoy relationships, and

I didn't have a challenge speaking to people, including women. To me, conversation with a member of the opposite gender isn't a big deal. My personality is such that I talk, have fun, and kid around, but none of it is serious. Unfortunately, engaging in these cultural practices in a place like Kota, however, led to misunderstandings, and false accusations and some difficult times for Sunita and me. Faithfulness to my wife was never up for debate, though, and my wife never questioned my fidelity. I am grateful that she stood by me the entire time as I took heat. She believed me and stuck with me, and I am so happy for that.

I was also well-liked by Dr. M.A. Thomas and Dr. Samuel Thomas (the misunderstanding regarding my wedding had been resolved), and as a result I continued to advance upward in my posts. I think there were those who disliked me for it, and that contributed to the slander I faced. But the Drs. Thomas also supported me in the midst of the attacks, and to this day I am grateful for it. I've always believed that God shakes our lives to keep us aware of where we are going.

I started teaching again in the Bible College, and began to take on different responsibilities concerning Emmanuel Orphanage. Being able to work with the orphanage where I grew up was one of the things I most enjoyed. In between that and teaching, I also began to take trips to Mumbai to minister to street kids.

When I returned to the streets of Mumbai, grown up, changed, now a young man of God with a family, I finally understood. And it was at this moment that I wept - wept for the seven years of my life spent on those very roads. Little did I know that God would use those experiences, many of which I am not proud of, to enable me to relate to and touch children similar to me, and all for His glory. Praise God.

"And we know that for those who love God all things work together for good, for those who are called according to his purpose. For those whom he foreknew he also predestined to be conformed to the image of his Son, in order that he might be the firstborn among many brothers. And those whom he predestined he also called, and those whom he called he also justified, and those whom he justified he also glorified.

What then shall we say to these things? If God is for us, who can be against us? He who did not spare his own Son but gave him up for us all, how will he not also with him graciously give us all things? Who shall bring any charge against God's elect? It is God who justifies. Who is to condemn? Christ Jesus is the one who died - more than that, who was raised - who is at the right hand of God, who indeed is interceding for us. Who shall separate us from the love of Christ? Shall tribulation, or distress, or persecution, or famine, or nakedness, or danger, or sword? As it is written, 'For your sake we are being killed all the day long; we are regarded as sheep to be slaughtered.' No, in all these things we are more than conquerors through him who loved us. For I am sure that neither death nor life, nor angels nor rulers, nor things present nor things to come, nor powers, nor height nor depth, nor anything else in all creation, will be able to separate us from the love of God in Christ Jesus our Lord."–

Romans 8:28-39

Chapter 11: Abraham

While at Emmanuel, Sunita became pregnant with our first child. I was excited and afraid at the same time. God was blessing me with my own family, but I wondered what kind of father I would be since I never knew mine.

I hoped we would have a girl because I had always wanted one. This desire was unusual, because in Indian culture, boys are usually wanted more than girls. But, because I had had experience working with female feticide and infanticide, I saw the ways in which girls in my country are treated unequally. They are often considered as others' property. Yet girls are precious. I have seen this in my own life. Girls are the ones who stand with you; they are the ones who will give you a glass of water on your dying bed.

I knew we would name our daughter Angie. Sunita and I have a good friend by the name of Angie Ellis who lives in Georgia now, but used to come to India regularly. She came to visit us when Sunita was pregnant, and up to that time we had been praying to God for a girl. "Lord God, we need a girl, we need a girl, we need a girl," I kept saying to the Lord, because in India it is illegal to find out the gender of the baby before it's born. When Angie told us about her visit, I told her, "Bring girls' clothes. We are having a girl." We also told her that we would name the baby Angie when it comes, because we liked her so much as a person.

God, however, had other plans.

When the time came for Sunita to have the baby, I was in the delivery room with her, even though this isn't generally allowed in Emmanuel Hospital in Kota. Sunita was having difficulty with the delivery; she was pushing, but the baby wasn't coming. The doctor finally realized that the umbilical cord was doubled around the baby's neck, and if the baby came out like that, it would strangle itself.

The doctor decided that it would be best to do a cesarean, but the procedure required my signature. At first I didn't want to give my consent, because even though the signing of the liability papers was just a formality, I was still scared. I didn't want to lose my wife. I loved Sunita so much. She was such a good wife, living a life of faith with me, standing by me through so much difficulty, even though people thought she was crazy to do so. They told her I would run away, that I wouldn't stay with her. But she made the choice and she stayed with me, so I was going to stay with her.

Finally, I told Sunita's uncle, Emmanuel Marandi, who worked in that very hospital, along with Sunita's auntie, to sign it. I couldn't do it. So they signed it, and Sunita went in for surgery.

I couldn't stay at the hospital and wait for it to be over, though. I had to relieve pressure. So I ran out, got on my motorcycle, and raced through the streets. Not long after, I got a call from a young woman named Lina, whom I think of as a younger sister, and who also worked at the hospital. "Bhaiya," she said. "God has given you a son."

When I heard that, I sped up on my motorcycle and it leapt in the air. I was so happy, I didn't even go back to see my son right away. I first went to the local shop and ordered sweets for all of the orphan children in Emmanuel Orphanage - nearly 2,000 children. After I'd gone and given sweets to every child, I then went back the hospital and took my son in my arms. For my wife and me, every celebration begins and ends with the orphan children.

Sunita and I gave our son the name "Abraham," after Dr. M.A. Thomas's father. He was a wonderful man who lived past 100 years of age, and at the time Sunita was giving birth in the hospital, he was in a hospital bed not too far from her. There in his hospital bed, as he approached the end of his life, he just sang praise and worship songs. I was so inspired by his testimony, and by the work of his son and grandson, that I decided to name my son after this great man of our Great Lord.

I couldn't have been happier that Abraham was born to us. Even though we had initially wanted a girl, God blessed us with a boy first. So we thanked the Lord, and prayed, "God, whenever you are ready for us to have a girl child, whether through birth or adoption, we will keep the name 'Angie' for her." Down the road, God would answer our prayer, for our second child would end up being a girl.

After being an orphan, I cried when I became a father. All those times I prayed to God as a boy, saying, "God, why don't I have a family?" Yet God brought many people in my life to serve as my family - as parents, brothers and sisters. Now God had given me the blessing of a child of my own, and finally I understood what it felt like to be a father. I cried a lot.

God does nothing wrong. Everything He does has a plan, but He has also given us a free will, and He will never interfere with that. We must therefore always ask ourselves, what is our level of surrender to God? If we surrender halfway, He will use us halfway. But if we surrender completely, He will use us completely.

"Every good gift and every perfect gift is from above, coming down from the Father of lights with whom there is no variation or shadow due to change. Of his own will he brought us forth by the word of truth, that we should be a kind of first fruits of his creatures."—James 1:17-18

Chapter 12: Varanasi

After Abraham was born, Sunita and I were privileged to go with another ministry (not associated with Emmanuel) to Varanasi, known as the holiest city in India. Many monks live there, and may people bring their dead to be burned and their ashes placed there. Hindus believe that if you die in Varanasi, you will go straight to heaven.

I began working in Varanasi with kids who lived on the city streets and on the platforms of two prominent railway stations: Varanasi and Mughalsarai. We worked there for a year and a half, then our second child - Angie - was born.

Even though it was a hard decision, after she was born my wife and I decided to leave Varanasi. I dropped her and the two children off by her family in Bihar, while I went to Delhi to look for a secular job. By that time, Sunita and I had be serving in formal ministry for years, and now that we had a young family, we figured it was time for a break, and that perhaps God was leading us elsewhere. I decided to go into the work field, and Sunita and I committed to doing whatever we could do for the Lord with whatever money we earned.

"The heart of man plans his way, but the LORD establishes his steps." -Proverbs 16:9

Chapter 13: Call Center Then Called Back

I went to Delhi and found a job in the call center, handling calls outsourced from America. So I rented a small home, sent for Sunita and the children, and began working and living in Delhi.

It was during that time that Emmanuel Ministries began to undergo severe persecution. While I had been a part of the ministry, there had been instances of opposition against Emmanuel that I had experienced, but by the time Sunita and I had gone from our life in Varanasi to Delhi, an arrest warrant had been issued for the Drs. Thomas because they had been accused of speaking against the Hindu god. They were now in hiding.

When I heard that Dr. M.A. and Samuel Thomas were in hiding, my wife and I went to see them. When we got to where they were, Dr. M.A. Thomas said to me, "God wants you to be in ministry, Alex. Come back to Kota."

So my family and I left Delhi and went back to Kota, and again I started teaching in the Bible College. I also began taking on greater responsibilities in the ministry.

During that time, however, I still wasn't sure what God wanted me to do. "God," am I on the right path?" I prayed. "Am I in the right place?"

Many times, God speaks through His people, and God used the Drs. Thomas to speak to me.

"You can't run away from God, Alex," Dr. Samuel Thomas said. "Do you think that it's just mere problems and difficulties you are running from? Think about us. Think about what we are facing." Before this incident, Dr. Samuel Thomas had already served 45 days in jail for the faith.

I thought for a long time about what he said, and it was true. So Sunita and I threw all of our energy into helping Emmanuel - teaching, assisting, visiting different parts of the country to build churches - and we did many other things in between. After we had worked there for a few years, up until 2007, Sunita and I began to feel that God might be calling us to go and start a ministry on our own.

"Many are the plans in the mind of a man, but it is the purpose of the LORD that will stand."–Proverbs 19:21

Chapter 14: Pakur

When Sunita and I felt this prompting of the Holy Spirit, we started praying about it. Meanwhile, we began thinking about where God might want us to go. I asked some people, and a few of them said, "Why don't you consider Pakur?"

"Pakur?" I said. "I don't know anything about Pakur."

So I did some research online and discovered that Pakur was a tribal region in Jharkhand, and the least literate district in India. It is one of the Santhal Pargana, serving as the geographical center for the Santhal, the largest tribal group in India. There were high levels of child trafficking taking place in the region as well.

As I read the statistics, I felt in my heart that this was where God was leading. It was a hard decision to make, though, because Dr. Samuel Thomas didn't want me to leave the ministry. He told me that I could always work there, and to be honest, at Emmanuel, I had everything I wanted. The people there stood with me in the time of trouble, loved me, and provided for me all the things I needed. Every time Dr. Samuel Thomas took a trip abroad, he would bring something back for my family. Two or three times after I'd decided that it was time for my family to leave Kota, I rethought it decided not to leave. I wasn't able to shake the call of

God though. Finally, one day, I resigned from the ministry, Sunita and I packed up our bags and our kids, the people at Emmanuel prayed for us, and sent us on our way to Jharkhand.

I looked into a few places to live in Pakur; but, like Jonah, instead of committing to go, I decided to go and have a look at Ranchi, the capital and metropolitan center of Jharkhand. I left my wife and kids again in Bihar with her family, because I didn't want her to have to be running here and there with the children without being settled. I went on my own to secure a place for us to stay.

Ranchi seemed great. Being the capital of Jharkhand, it had malls, and shops, and all the luxuries of middle class life. I even went and saw a home. It was nice, and would be perfect for us. So I secured it with a deposit, and just like that everything was done and settled for us to begin a ministry in Ranchi.

We had left our luggage in Kota, at Emmanuel, until I could secure a home for us. So, upon settling things in Ranchi, I wrote to the ministry and asked that they send our things to us. But, I accidentally gave them the wrong address. Without even realizing it, I gave them an address to one of the places I had been looking at in Pakur rather than the home I'd secured in Ranchi! So, all of my family's belongings were sent to an address in Pakur, even though I'd never been there.

There I was: home ready in Ranchi, all of our belongings in Pakur. Even though I had accidentally sent our things to Pakur, it was no mistake but God's doing, because I knew in my heart that Ranchi wasn't right. Ranchi was easier, because it was the city, where you can get everything - Pepsi and ice cream whenever you please - and it wasn't hard for me to agree to the rent there because of how much easier that would be. But it wasn't where God wanted us.

So I went to Pakur. I secured the room of the address I had "accidentally" given to the people in Kota and then sent for my family in Bihar. Lucky for us, our luggage was already waiting for us at our new home.

Transitioning to life in Pakur was just what I'd thought it would be: hard. When we went shopping, there was hardly anything to buy. We couldn't find any of the things we were looking for, and there was definitely no Pepsi or ice cream.

"God, am I in the right place?" I pleaded. Because if not, I had enough money to go back to Ranchi. I ended up finding a college close to where we lived, however, that needed someone to teach English to youths. I told them that I could teach English, as I had a good amount of teaching experience, and so I became employed by the college.

For one whole year, Sunita and I wrestled with the question of whether God really wanted us to stay in

Pakur. As I started teaching I began to earn money, and that provided some relief to me, as my family and I began to find our footing. We also found a large supermarket five hours away by train that had all of the things we could not get locally, so we were able to take that trip when necessary and find what we needed.

God wanted us to stay in Pakur. Amen.

"And the LORD will guide you continually and satisfy
your desire in scorched places and make your bones
strong;
and you shall be like a watered garden,
like a spring of water, whose waters do not fail.
And your ancient ruins shall be rebuilt;
You shall raise up the foundations of many generations;
You shall be called the repairer of the breach,
The restorer of streets to dwell in."–Isaiah 58:11-12

Chapter 15: Orphans

With the money I began earning teaching English, we dove right in, began a Vacation Bible School (VBS) and did as much as we could with the money provided. This was the beginning of the Lord's youth ministry through us.

Then, one day, a local man came to me. "Sir," he said, "There is a boy wandering in the village. He has no parents. Some days he eats, some days he doesn't."

Sunita and I always had a heart for orphan children, so I said to the man, "Bring him to me." I thought to myself, no problem, one child can eat with us. A few weeks later, two more children came. Even though Sunita and my rooms were small, we now have five children with us - our two and three orphans. By the time the sixth child came, Martina, we decided to start a school.

Sunita and I thanked God, for He showed Himself to be gracious to us. He had begun to fulfill our dream of being able to care for orphan children. My only stipulation in taking in a child was that the child had to be a real orphan without any parent living. The reason for this is because I understand how hard it is on a child to be separated from family. I missed my family, and so did my wife. Even though they were living, she had to live without them for many years, and parental love can't be replaced. That is why I prefer to help a child in the context of his or her environment and family life: I believe that parents and children should not be separated. In starting a school and offering free education, it was Sunita and my desire to facilitate keeping families together where possible, and relieve the burden placed on poor parents to choose between educating their children and keeping them. When we started the first school, I only had a small amount of savings, which I withdrew to buy benches for the classroom; now God has established two schools through our efforts, both of which are officially registered with the government today. Praise the Lord.

God has truly blessed us. Today, along with Abraham and Angie, our two biological kids, Grace, our adopted daughter, and nine orphan children: Prabhu, Luke, Basanti, Martina, Raja, Mampi, Mamta, Hakim and Allison. These children live with us and eat around our table. I believe strongly in family environment, because that is what the orphan longs for: family.

Even though all of the orphans living with us are without parents, a few of them have distant relatives. So we don't require that they call us "mother" and "father" because while we love them as though they came from us, we understand that we are their foster parents. We are their Uncle and Auntie. In light of that, it is Sunita and my intent to raise them up in God then send them back to their communities as living testimonies of God's faithfulness, taking the Gospel with them. That is our desire.

But oh, how I love children. I love them very much. The Lord knows, if I have nothing to my name in this world, just give me a child and I will be content.

Children are everything to me. As I said before, everything significant in my life begins and ends with a child.

"At that time the disciples came to Jesus, saying, 'Who is the greatest in the kingdom of heaven?' And calling to him a child, he put him in the midst of them and said, 'Truly, I say to you, unless you turn and become like children, you will never enter the kingdom of heaven. Whoever humbles himself like this child is the greatest in the kingdom of heaven.
Whoever receives one such child in my name receives me, but whoever causes one of these little ones who believe in me to sin, it would be better for him to have a great millstone fastened around his neck and to be drowned in the depth of the sea...see that you do not despise one of these little ones. For I tell you that in heaven their angels always see the face of my Father who is in heaven."—Matthew 18:1-6, 10

Chapter 16: The Body of Christ

In India, there is a caste system in which there are different castes: high caste, middle caste, and low caste. The Brahmins are the "head," representative of knowledge; they comprise the religious priesthood and are the ones who perform the important rituals and such. Next come Kshatriya (or Rajput), the "shoulders," and they are made up of kings, rulers, administrators and those who govern. Vaishya, the "hip," are business owners, farmers and traders; Shudra, the "legs and feet," clean toilets and provide services to the higher castes, and the foot is never to be on the head. And then there are the Dalits, or "untouchables." They aren't even considered part of the body. Even though Shudras are part of the feet, they are still part of the body. Dalits aren't even seen as people.

Dalits aren't allowed in the homes of the people of higher castes, and when they walk on the street, they must remove their slippers and put them on top of their head. And if a higher caste person passes on the road or is sitting alongside it, Dalits must bow low and not even look at them.

It is terrible, and I don't enjoy speaking of it. For in God's eyes, all have sinned and fall short of the glory of God; in that we are all equal. Therefore, the way to salvation is the same for all: through Jesus Christ. "I am the Way, and the Truth, and the Life," Jesus said. "No one comes to the Father except through me." (John 14:6) This is the truth that governs the work of the Lord in the ministry He has given us. For in the Kingdom of God, there is no place for such divisions. Neither is there place for it in our orphanage.

In our orphanage, all of the children, regardless of background, are raised as brothers and sisters. In the Northeastern region of India, in Manipur and Nagaland, there has been a longstanding history of brutal conflict between two groups of people: the Kuki and the Naga. There was a point in time when they were fighting every day, killing each other and burning each other's homes. Yet, in our orphanage, we have Naga and Kuki living under the same roof as friends.

Jharkhand, being a tribal state, has many different tribes of people: those who live in the mountains, those who live in the country, and so on. In my home, however, the Malto, Cora and Santhal tribes are all represented, living as family, even as there remain so many reasons and so many systems that continue to divide the people of India. It is absolutely amazing and wonderful to see. For as Paul wrote to the church in Corinth, in Christ's body, there is no division:

> For just as the body is one and has many members, and all the members of the body, though many, are one body, so it is with Christ. For in one Spirit we were all baptized into one body - Jews or Greeks, slaves or free - and all were made to drink of one Spirit.
>
> For the body does not consist of one member but of many. If the foot should say, "Because I am not a hand, I do not belong to the body," that would not make it any less a part of the body. And if the ear should say, "Because I am not an eye, I do not belong to the body," that would not make it any less a part of the body. If the whole body were an eye, where would be the sense of hearing? If the whole body were an ear, where would be the sense of smell? But as it is, God

arranged the members in the body, each one of them, as he chose. If all were a single member, where would the body be? As it is, there are many parts, yet one body. The eye cannot say to the hand, "I have no need of you," nor again the head to the feet, "I have no need of you." On the contrary, the parts of the body that seem to be weaker are indispensable, and on those parts of the body that we think less honorable we bestow the greater honor, and our un-presentable parts are treated with greater modesty, which our more presentable parts do not require. But God has so composed the body, giving greater honor to the part that lacked it, that there may be no division in the body, but that the members may have the same care for one another. If one member suffers, all suffer together; if one member is honored, all rejoice together.

-1 Corinthians 12:12-27.

Chapter 17: Everett Mission

The ministry the Lord began through us in Pakur is called Everett Mission today, and God continues to bless it. We have an orphan home - Sunita and my home is the orphan home - with nine orphan children now a part of our family. We have two schools that educate children of all economic and social backgrounds, and offer free education and school supply sponsorship for students who cannot afford to pay the school fees. Whatever money we get, we apply it to the needs, and God continues to bring us new friends and partners.

During school holidays, we are busy running youth camps in Jharkhand and Bihar, as well as VBS and spiritual conferences for children. By 2014, we hope to be able to expand our two youth camps to three, and all in different states. We are working on it and praying about it.

The Lord has also given me a local home church that I pastor - even though I see myself as every other laborer in the Kingdom. This has provided the opportunity, however, to visit many other churches, domestically and abroad, and to preach and teach and share what God is doing in our midst.

Living by faith is our daily walk at Everett Mission. When it comes to the orphanage, home rent and things like groceries, many times I don't know how our needs are going to be met. Add to that the needs of the community, which include things like blankets and shoes and additional food supplies. Yet God has always provided. With the money we get from our schools, with my occasional teaching engagements with students studying English, along with the money God brings from members of the church all over the world, our needs are met daily.

To God be the glory!

"And my God will supply every need of yours according to his riches in glory in Christ Jesus. To our God and Father be glory forever and ever. Amen."
—Philippians 4:19-20

Chapter 18: Down the Road

The tribal community with which we work in Pakur only yields one crop a year; in other places, it is customary to have three or four in a year. In Pakur, however, because of the water crises and problems with flooding, many people rely on coals for food - coals that fall off the fuel trucks in passing or that can be secretly gleaned. Those they gather and sell. That is one of their primary sources for making a living. Pakur is also known for its stones, which are used to make concrete and pave roads. People therefore take such gravel, grind it, and sell it to people making terraces and roads and such.

For this reason, Everett Mission would like to start its own small-scale industries, such as making candles, stitching clothes, and even starting a chain of health gyms. This would benefit the community not only in helping it (and the ministry) become more self-sustained, but in raising the standard of living. We don't want to go into business just for the financial benefits it would provide to us. We want to bring jobs to poor people in the community so that they can stay away from prostitution and other unwanted things in life. They would be able to work in their villages, and support themselves and their families with dignity.

Working in Pakur, we see the needs of the people every day. We therefore hope that God will enable us to establish local industries that can pay a competitive, respectable wage to workers. It would offer much-needed employment opportunities to the people who are earning less than one US Dollar a day, those who don't have work at all, or those who need a part-time means of support. This arrangement would be ideal for many women in the community who have a desire to take care of their children and send them to school, but who also have responsibilities at home to their husbands and households. They would be able, in their free time, to work for our ministry, whether it be making candles, or eatable treats for the children, or sewing clothes, etc. Then, building a few fitness facilities in the area would be great for the youths, because they would be able to spend their free time in a healthy, positive environment and keep off the streets.

There is also the dream of establishing more family-oriented orphanages for children. I hope to continue to bring greater awareness to Indian churches of the need to adopt children into their families. It can be done, and many have the means to do it. It is also biblical, for we, being spiritually orphaned, were adopted by God into His family. The adoption of children, therefore, would be His demonstration of love to us expressed through us.

Finally, I have a desire to start a project in Mumbai. There are so many street vendors in the city - people selling things at traffic signals, railway stations, on bridges, everywhere - with families they are struggling to support. I therefore would like to take the children of such vendors, establish a school in Mumbai (so they wouldn't be separated from their families) and educate them. If we have the means to board them at school, they would still have open and frequent access to their families and homes, and their parents would be able to visit them once a week or once a day -

whichever suits them. Yet the burden of education would be removed from the parents as would the price they would have to pay in sending their children away. This is a dream of mine. If it is God's will, it will happen.

For now, though, my work is with the town to which I am called - Pakur - and to the children God has given me. My wife and I made a commitment long ago that we won't take any property in our name. We won't take any salary from the ministry, or from the church we pastor, nor will we ever have a ministry bank account in our names. If God so chooses to bless us with a small business, then yes, we would like to have at least a home for our children. But I will not make ministry into a family business. Service to the Lord is about calling, and I believe people should only end up in ministry if they are truly called. And when you are called, the Lord will take care of you and of His ministry, for He always finishes what He starts. Understanding that Sunita and

I are merely stewards of Everett Mission is very important to us, and we pray that we never get sidetracked from the truth of these things or forget them.

"Blessed are you, O LORD, the God of Israel our father, forever and ever. Yours, O LORD, is the greatness and the power and the glory and the victory and the majesty, for all that is in the heavens and in the earth is yours. Yours is the kingdom, O LORD, and you are exalted as head above all. Both riches and honor come from you, and you rule over all. In your hand are power and might, and in your hand it is to make great and to give strength to all. And now we thank you, our God, and praise your glorious name.
But who am I, and what is my people, that we should be able thus to offer willingly? For all things come from you, and of your own have we given you. For we are strangers before you and sojourners, as all our fathers were. Our days on the earth are like a shadow, and

there is no abiding. O LORD our God, all this abundance that we have provided for building you a house for your holy name comes from your hand and is all your own."—1 Chronicles 29:10b-16

Chapter 19: Thy Kingdom Come

Here at Everett Mission, more than money, we seek friends and partners who will share their talents and prayers with our community. Orphan children have people who will give them food; they are looking for people to love them. I longed for it in my own life, many times when I was on the roads of Mumbai. We pray that God continues to bring us such people.

I do not believe that one in ministry should be going after money. It is necessary, yes, but if you have the faith, God will provide for His own. Loving money, seeking it with our hearts, however - that is the root of all evil.

As I mentioned before, Everett Mission wants to become self-sufficient so that we are not only able to help our ministry, but also the ministries of others. There are many other ministries that don't have Facebook status, a website or even an email address, yet they are doing tremendous work for the Kingdom of God, ground level, grassroots, with their own money. For the mission is in their hearts. Therefore, I encourage people to come and visit us, but I will also take them to other ministries so that if they want to give, they can be a blessing to other laborers of the Kingdom also.

I have seen many things in my time in ministry, and some of them are discouraging, and remain a struggle for me. Many Christian leaders begin at the bottom: humble, with nothing, and they call themselves "poor pastors," "poor servants," "poor leaders." It is then that they identify with the poor and lowly of the earth.

As material blessings come, however, and their ministries expand, and they get a thriving orphanage, they move from scratch cars to luxury cars, from local schooling for their own children to international private schooling in America and other places, traveling here and there in comfort. Yet the orphan children in their care are still orphans, still struggling for higher education, still looking for someone to come and help them. In light of this, and seeing the number of people who don't have enough food to eat on a daily basis, I don't understand how you can call yourself a follower of

Jesus, see that need, and still go spend lots of money on a car, or a big estate, or a luxurious office. I don't understand these things. But as my wife always says, there will be a day of reckoning when our deeds are called into account. For there will be those to whom Jesus will say, "Depart from me, for I never knew you."

May God keep us from such temptations.

"When the Son of Man comes in his glory, and all the angels with him, then he will sit on his glorious throne. Before him will be gathered all the nations, and he will separate people one from another as a shepherd separates the sheep from the goats. And he will place the sheep on his right, but the goats on the left. Then the King will say to those on his right, 'Come, you who are blessed by my father, inherit the kingdom prepared for you from the foundation of the world. For I was hungry and you gave me food, I was thirsty and you gave me drink, I was a stranger and you welcomed me,

I was naked and you clothed me, I was sick and you visited me, I was in prison and you came to me.' Then the righteous will answer him, saying, 'Lord, when did we see you hungry and feed you, or thirsty and give you drink? And when did we see you a stranger and welcome you, or naked and clothe you? And when did we see you sick or in prison and visit you? And the King will answer them, 'Truly, I say to you, as you did it to one of the least of these my brothers, you did it to me.'"–Matthew 25:31-40

Chapter 20: Final Words

I believe God called me as He did because there is a need, and someone has to be a voice. If you had malaria and recovered, you can tell others how to treat it because you know how it was treated in you. I therefore believe that God allowed me to go through the situations I went through because even when I didn't know it, He was working them together for my good, as Romans 8:28 says.

In writing this book, only two things have been my desire: that with each page you see the merciful hand of God at work in my life, and that you know that no matter how unworthy or abandoned a life is, God can change that precious life for His glory. God changes people for His kingdom, and He can use even the worst of us as a living testimony of His faithfulness. I can attest to this, because Jesus completely changed my life.

Is this my message? No, this is God's message. I am just the messenger.

> "I waited patiently for the LORD;
> He inclined to me and heard my cry.
> He drew me up from the pit of destruction,
> Out of the miry bog,
> and set my feet upon a rock,

making my steps secure.

He put a new song in my mouth,

a song of praise to our God.

Many will see and fear,

and put their trust in the LORD.

Blessed is the man who makes the LORD his trust,

Who does not turn to the proud,

to those who go astray after a lie!

You have multiplied, O LORD my God,

your wondrous deeds and your thoughts toward us;

none can compare with you!

I will proclaim and tell of them,

yet they are more than can be told."–Psalms 40:1-5

Amen.